I0756867

Meet a little bunny, his name is Manny.

He loved to jump high when the day was sunny.

But this day he was making noises that were very funny!

What was that sound? Asked little Manny.

Farts were the answer, to the question of bunny!

Manny, a little bunny sniffed once:
SNIFF
BLOOOF!

Then twice:
SNIFF
SNIFF
TOOOT!

Oh no! It smells like a pooping
mice!

My friends are going to call
me gross,

beacuse my pooper goes:
SMOOF!
BLOOFY!
TOOT!

Manny, dont worry, he heard
a voice.

First our bunny got scared,
then he made a choice.

I am going to check what is
that voice!

A few farts later, he got to the point.

BRRRT!
PRRRF!

It occured its a Clever Parrot called Piper that first took off her diaper.

Manny was very surprised.

You heard my farts why wont You call me Manny the farting Bunny?

A Clever Parrot called Piper that first took off her diaper responded.

Because its normal, to fart when you eat not a part but a whole cart of carrots and cabbages!

Oh no! Our little Manny got
sad.

Now I am going to fart for my whole life?

No Little Manny,

Your farts are going to end in
a blink of an eye!

That is awesome,

said Manny, but he jumped
too, farting so hard he could
fly like a cuckoo!

Sorry, said Bunny.

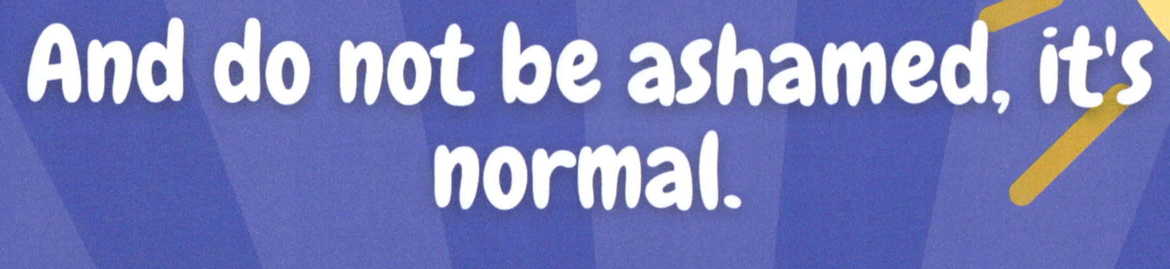
And do not be ashamed, it's normal.

Really? I can fart where and when I want?

Not really, Piper responded

Even me, Clever Parrot called Piper that first took off her diaper farts sometimes.

but ONLY in a right place in a right time!

Just remember, dont fart
near other people, go to the
nearest empty place
and release all farts You got!

Thank You so much Piper that
first took off her diaper!

Now I know how and where to fart!
SMOOF!
BRRRT!

After lesson so important,
Manny the farting Bunny
flew away farting funny!

But now knowing that
everybody is farting, even
the Clever Parrot
called Piper that first took
off her diaper, he was not
afraid that friends are going
to
call him a Farting Bunny.

THANKS FOR READING, CHECK
OUR OTHER BOOKS
THAT ARE GOING TO SHOW UP
ON OUR AMAZON AUTHOR
SITE!

Coconut Papers